THE 12% SOLUTION

Earn a 12% Average Annual Return on your Money,
Beating The S&P 500, Mad Money's Jim Cramer
and 99% of all Mutual Fund Managers...

By Making 2-4 Trades Per Month

David Alan Carter

READ THE DISCLAIMER BEFORE PROCEEDING

WITH THIS BOOK

ISBN-13: 978-1974681365
ISBN-10: 197468136X

Table of Contents

Chapter 1 - Why I Wrote This Book 5

Chapter 2 - Who Should Read This Book 7

Chapter 3 - The Buffett Bet 9

Chapter 4 - SPY and TLT: The Foundation 13

Chapter 5 - Building on the Foundation 25

Chapter 6 - A Cash Trigger 37

Chapter 7 - Building on the Foundation, Part II 43

Chapter 8 - The 12% Solution 51

Chapter 9 - OK, But Does an Extra 5% Really Matter? 57

Chapter 10 - Caveats and Q&A 61

A Note To The Reader 65

About The Author 67

Also By David Alan Carter 69

Appendix A: Brokers and Commissions 71

Appendix B: Disclaimer 75

Chapter 1 - Why I Wrote This Book

Don't be like me. More specifically, don't be like the younger me.

I wrote this book because of people like me. Because this is exactly the kind of advice I wish I had been given nineteen years ago. Back then, I was brimming with confidence that I would be able to figure out this stock market thing, game the system, power invest my way into an early retirement. That was in 1998. And in fact, after an initial period of brutal losses, I began piling up profitable trades and my brokerage account began to grow -- impressively. Yes, of course, I was a genius.

Then 2000 happened. The Dot-Com Crash. From peak to bottom, the Nasdaq Composite lost 78% of its value. I went from genius to doofus practically overnight. In the back of my mind was this thought: squirrel away a set of flatware so that I might be able to eat with some dignity out of a dumpster.

But in time I recovered. Then the market downturn of 2002 happened. After a few months of rice and pintos, again I pulled my account up by its bootstraps. Then it was the collapse of the Chinese stock bubble of 2007. Then the financial crisis of 2007-2009 (The Great Recession). The European sovereign debt crisis of 2010. The Flash Crash of the same year. The market selloff of 2015-2016.

Each time I eventually recovered. And each time I listened to more gurus, watched more CNBC, experimented with more bizarre technical charting patterns and developed new and improved investment strategies.

And when it was all said and done? After 18 years of countless hours of toil and trades, stress and sleepless nights, I was only marginally ahead. It was a rare year that I beat the popular benchmark, The S&P 500. More often, I lagged behind that benchmark – sometimes far behind.

In 2016, while researching yet another foolproof trading strategy, I stumbled across an obscure article on the subject of sector rotation. It got me thinking. And the more I thought, the more a strategy began to crystallize.

I wrote this book because of people like me. Because this is exactly the kind of advice I wish I had been given nineteen years ago.

Chapter 2 - Who Should Read This Book

First off, let me state that this book will not appeal to every investor. Nor should it. There will be those investors who have either stumbled upon or have carefully researched a fund or combination of funds that have produced a satisfactory level of returns. To those individuals, my hat's off to you and I wish you the best of luck.

Others might be active traders who have mastered a system by which they win more often than they lose, who enjoy what they're doing, and are building a career for themselves managing a fast-growing portfolio. To those, Godspeed.

Finally, there are investors who don't wish to deal with the tax implications of trading monthly; for some, especially high net worth individuals, a buy-and-hold strategy assuring only long-term capital gains at tax time is preferable to beating the S&P 500 by a few points. (TIP: Implement the strategy in a tax-deferred or tax-exempt retirement account.)

So who is this book for? Pretty much everybody else. It's for those who are just starting out in stock market investing and overwhelmed with the choices. It's for those who have spent a few years moving in and out of individual stocks or mutual funds or ETFs, chasing returns or following the advice of money managers or market gurus only to be disappointed at the end of each year.

It's for those who have money on the line in such risky bets that they can't sleep at night. It's for those who want to be invested but live in fear of the next dot-com bubble burst or Great Recession when the U.S. stock market lost 57% of its value. It's for those willing to sacrifice a little larger tax bite in traditional brokerage accounts (short-term capital gains vs. long-term capital gains) in exchange for up to 5% annually in additional investment returns.

It's for anybody who isn't currently generating an average 12% annually on their investments, and wants to be. And wants some modicum of assurance that they won't get wiped out in the process.

In clear, precise terms, I lay out a blueprint for achieving annual returns that – over the past 10 years – have outperformed the S&P 500, the gold-standard benchmark for U.S. stock market performance. And while the most often repeated of investment advice – past performance is no guarantee of future results – remains valid, the reader can judge for himself as to the logic behind the strategy, and the likelihood of outperformance going forward.

To those new at stock market investing, becoming actively involved in the direction and velocity of your portfolio may seem frightening, like working a lot of moving parts on a piece of machinery traveling along at an unsafe speed on a road with no guardrails. I understand this completely, and want you to know that I developed this strategy with two primary concerns: 1) simplicity, and 2) safety.

I wanted anybody and everybody to be able to follow this plan easily and with simple tools that are readily available at no charge; no need to lash yourself to onerous software or be a mathematics genius. And I wanted guardrails firmly in place along the road. That's not to say I've eliminated the risk associated with stock market investing. That's simply not possible, and those who require an absolutely risk-free investing environment need to look elsewhere. But reducing risk in the form of volatility and drawdowns (peak-to-trough declines) has been a priority.

Although many if not most of my readers will be new to the stock market, I don't intend this book to be an intro into stock market investing. For the basics regarding selecting a brokerage firm, setting up a trading account, and executing trades, there are warehouses of books and the Internet at your disposal.

For those new to investing as well as those experienced to the point of frustration, I welcome you and congratulate you on taking this first step. Together, let's uncover a simple and logical approach to investing that automates the decision making, commands 20 minutes of your time per month, and helps you sleep like a baby during the most turbulent of markets.

It's been hiding in plain sight for years. You're going to kick yourself when you see how easy this is.

Welcome to *The 12% Solution*.

Chapter 3 - The Buffett Bet

When Warren Buffett speaks, people listen. Or do they?

Buffett is an American business magnate, investor, and philanthropist, and considered by many to be one of the most successful investors in the world. According to Wikipedia, as of March 2017 Buffett is the second wealthiest person in the United States with a total net worth of $73.3 billion.

As the Chief Executive of Berkshire Hathaway, the 4th largest company in the world, Buffett is known for dispensing financial wisdom from time to time. Often, some of that wisdom comes out in the annual Berkshire Hathaway letter to shareholders.

In the most recent such letter (2017), in a section titled "The Bet," Buffett revisited a wager he proposed back in 2007. Buffett bet that he could outperform any investment professional selecting a set of 5 or more hedge funds over a time span of 10 years. Hedge funds are investment funds catering to high-wealth individuals and institutional investors. They often use complex portfolio-construction and risk-management techniques – and charge high fees for their services.

Buffett's vehicle of choice for his side of the bet? One single mutual fund that simply tracks the S&P 500 index.

A single investment pro stepped forward at the time – Ted Seides, at the time the Asset Manager for the firm Protégé Partners. And the bet was on. The loser would write a check to charity.

With nine years down and one to go, Buffett looks virtually certain to win the bet. The fund Buffett picked, the Vanguard 500 Index Fund Admiral Share, has generated an average annual return of 7.1%. Protégé's fund of funds has returned 2.2%. That's a three to one beat down.

What happened? How could a simple fund that mimics the S&P 500 outperform high-priced professional money managers with tool bags brimming with proprietary research and sophisticated trading techniques?

As Buffett explains it, while there are some money managers with the chops to beat the market in any given year or even several years, those are rare birds. And those who do win inadvertently sow the seeds of future failure by attracting hoards of new money. While that sounds counterintuitive, managing a multi-million dollar portfolio is quite different than managing a multi-billion dollar portfolio.

Those high management fees certainly play a factor. If the S&P 500 returns 8% in a given year, the money manager charging his clients 2% annually has got to deliver a return of 10% just to match the benchmark index. Most simply can't do it, certainly not year after year for ten years.

Contrary to what money managers would like you to believe, multiple studies have confirmed that high management fees do not improve returns, indeed they are an impediment to returns.

So, what advice does Buffett give to stock market novices and mega-rich investors alike? Not surprisingly, he advises all to buy and hold a low-cost fund that tracks the S&P 500 index. It works, and he has study after study on his side and will soon have half a million dollars in winnings to accentuate the point.

But here's the surprising part: not everyone takes that advice. Some do – typically those stock market novices with little money to spare. But folks with the kind of money that can buy a high-fee manager, or those with a little bit of trading prowess or those easily infatuated with gurus of every stripe are often deaf to the advice.

Why? Gurus know how to lure. It has a lot to do with marketing and promotion. Every financial magazine touts the credentials of money managers who have beaten the street at one time or another. There are pages and pages filled with rankings of actively-managed mutual funds all competing for investor dollars. The corporate machinations and the ins and outs of top management are fodder for endless glowing articles that are often lacking in objectivity and read like they could have been written by the corporate communications teams themselves.

Cable news shows like CNBC offer up an endless parade of money managers touting this stock or that stock, and displaying such an in-depth understanding of markets and economics that the average viewer inevitably concludes that these brainiacs will make them far more money than passive investing. Viewers are swayed to trade on those stock recommendations themselves, or hand over their investable nest egg to the companies those brainiacs represent.

I know of what I speak. I spent 18 years generating subpar returns by hanging on every stock picking recommendation from the so-called experts, then giving up monies to mutual funds, then switching those funds around trying to chase returns, and then returning to frantic trading with my own accounts. Rinse and repeat for 18 years, and I've left a small fortune on the table by not following Buffett's simple advice.

Ah, the siren song of the rock-star money managers and the TV personalities with their stock-picking prowess and their one or two years of outrageous returns. Don't be swayed into chasing those returns. Over the long run, nothing much beats the unemotional, low-cost funds that mirror broad-market indices. That would be something like Buffett's choice of mutual fund, or ETFs -- Exchange Traded Funds.

But how do they work, and which funds or ETFs are we talking about? Let's go there. But first, to summarize…

THE BUFFETT BET
takeaways

> Study after study has shown that cutting your cost of investing is one of the most significant things you can do to improve your returns over time.
> It's a rare money manager who can beat the S&P 500 index in a given year, and even more rare to beat the street multiple years in a row.
> While there is a large industrial complex of television and print media that tries to instill reliance on master stock pickers as the way to go, a simple, inexpensive fund that mirrors a major market index like the S&P 500 most often wins in the long run.
> Don't bet against Warren Buffett.

Chapter 4 - SPY and TLT: The Foundation

In his bet, Warren Buffett's investment choice for tracking the S&P 500 index was the Vanguard 500 Index Fund Admiral Share, ticker symbol VFIAX. While this is a mutual fund, the expense ratio (read, management fees) are quite low by mutual fund standards: 0.09%. So that's good.

But because it's a mutual fund, buying and selling shares is subject to the peculiarities of the mutual fund industry. For example, unlike stocks and ETFs, mutual funds trade only once daily, after the markets close. You can place your buy or sell order at any time during the day, but the price associated with that trade will be calculated after the market closes and typically posted by 6:00 p.m. Eastern Time.

In addition, this particular fund can only be purchased through a Vanguard Brokerage Account or a Vanguard account that holds only Vanguard mutual funds.

SPY, THE "RISK-ON" TRADE

For *The 12% Solution*, we're looking for funds with wider availability and a greater flexibility of transaction. ETFs fit the bill, and in particular the SPDR ETF (Standard & Poor's depositary receipt exchange traded funds) that goes by the ticker symbol SPY.

Definitions:

> *An ETF, or exchange traded fund, is a marketable security that tracks an index, a commodity, bonds, or a basket of assets like an index fund. Unlike mutual funds, an ETF trades like a common stock on a stock exchange. ETFs experience price changes throughout the day as they are bought and sold. ETFs typically have higher daily liquidity and lower fees than mutual fund shares, making them an attractive alternative for individual investors. Because it trades like a stock, an ETF does not have its*

> *net asset value (NAV) calculated once at the end of every day like a mutual fund does. -- Source: Investopedia*
>
> *__SPDR funds__ are a family of exchange-traded funds (ETFs) traded in the United States, Europe, and Asia-Pacific and managed by State Street Global Advisors (SSGA). Informally, they are also known as Spyders or Spiders. The name is an acronym for Standard & Poor's Depositary Receipts. -- Source: Wikipedia*
>
> *__The SPDR S&P 500 trust__ is an exchange-traded fund which trades on the NYSE Arca under the symbol SPY. It is designed to track the S&P 500 stock market index. Each share of the SPY ETF holds a stake in the 500 stocks represented by the S&P 500 -- Source: Wikipedia and Investopedia*

From day one of its inception in 1993, SPY has been wildly popular as an investment vehicle. Buying SPY means buying a stake in each of the 500 companies that make up the Standard & Poor's index. These are large cap (large capitalization) companies selected by a team of analysts and economists at Standard & Poor's.

Collectively, the 500 stocks that make up the S&P 500 are widely regarded as the most accurate gauge of the large-cap sector of the American stock market and representative of the American stock market as a whole, so much so that the index has become one of the common benchmarks by which analysts and investors gauge the performance of everything from individual securities to mutual funds, sector and foreign markets, and money managers themselves.

So SPY, representing large-cap U.S. stocks, will become a key ingredient of *The 12% Solution*. In fact, for those investors content to generate the kind of returns Warren Buffet received during the course of his infamous bet, simply buying and holding SPY will get you there. Specifically, +7.06% average annual return for the past ten years (vs. +7.15% for Buffett's mutual fund selection, the Vanguard 500 Index Fund Admiral Class, ticker symbol VFIAX).

There's certainly nothing shabby about a 7% average annual return, and in fact with that return you'd be besting the great majority of money managers, stock market analysts and TV personalities.

But what if we could boost that respectable return with a little bit of tinkering?

One of the first things you'll notice if you look at a long-term chart of SPY is that it does correlate exactly with the U.S. stock market (i.e., the S&P 500). That's both good and bad. Good – when the market is on a tear upward. Bad – when all hell breaks loose and the bottom falls out of the market.

In the latter camp, a couple of notable bear markets include the bursting of the dot-com bubble in 2000-2002 (over 30 months, the S&P 500 lost 49.1%), and the bursting of the housing bubble in 2007-2009 (over 17 months, the S&P 500 lost 56.4%).

Now, over time, the index and associated ETFs like SPY recovered. And then some. So all is well, right?

Not exactly. If you had been approaching retirement in 2001 or 2008, watching your hard-earned nest egg cut in half right before you're handed your gold watch would be devastating at the least. It's not enough to "know" that the market would bounce back eventually. If you needed cash from stocks during those down years, for whatever reason, you're selling at significant losses. If you'd bought on margin, you could face liquidation.

Even if you don't *need* to sell, watching retirement and brokerage accounts evaporate to that extent plays hard on the emotions of most people. All too many end up selling on panic, taking significant losses, and are then too afraid to get back into stocks as the market begins to claw its way back up.

So there they sit, with less money than they started, swearing off the stock market and stuffing what little dollars they have left into passbook savings accounts or mattresses.

It's hard to blame them. But the stock market is the place to be if you want your money to generate money. And most people don't get rich, or even comfortably well off, without their money generating money. But is there a way to mitigate losses during stock market downturns?

HEDGING THE RISK

There is. And there's a term for it: hedging. A hedge is an investment that -- in theory -- reduces the risk of adverse price movements in an asset. We hedge in many aspects of our life, though most people never look at it in quite that context.

Home insurance, for example. We pay monthly or annual premiums for insurance that will reimburse us in the event of catastrophic damage to our home. By protecting our home (and car, and health, and life) with insurance policies, we are employing the principle of hedging.

Hedging is simply a technique for reducing or transferring risk. Understand, though, that there is almost always a price associated with a hedge. In the case of homeowners insurance, the price is the monthly or annual premiums we pay – regardless of whether or not we'll ever have a tree go through the roof and receive a payout from that policy.

In the stock market, the cost of hedging usually manifests itself as lower returns than if you "bet the farm" on a volatile stock or basket of stocks with no such protection.

Hedges can involve derivatives (i.e. options, swaps, futures and forward contracts) based on the underlying asset in question. OK, that can be complicated. But a hedge can also be an offsetting position in a security that tends to move in an inverse relationship to the one being hedged. That sounds simpler, and as luck would have it, just so happens to be the direction we're going to move in.

Among assets that tend to move in inverse relationship to the broader market (for which SPY represents) are several that have become commonplace in the tool bags of savvy investors. They include gold, silver and other precious metals, utility stocks, and bonds. When the stock market as a whole turns south, gold and other precious metals often – but not always – turn north. When the markets move higher, gold and precious metals often – but not always – move lower. Ditto with utility stocks.

But notice this isn't a perfect inverse relationship. During the housing crash and subsequent recession of 2007-2009, gold and utilities followed the overall market right down into the abyss. Bonds are a bit more predictable as a hedge against common stocks, with treasuries leading the pack in this respect.

In fact, while there are a number of negatively correlated components of the overall financial market, perhaps none is more resilient and widely accepted than that of the stock market and bonds (U.S. treasuries in particular).

Let's consider treasuries in more depth. And in keeping with our focus on simplicity of strategy and ease of execution, we'll look specifically at the asset TLT. But first...

Definitions:

> *Treasuries, or treasury bonds or securities, are debt obligations of a national government. United States Treasury securities, therefore, are debt obligations of the United States government and are issued to finance the national debt of the United States. Because U.S. treasuries are backed by the full faith, credit and taxing power of the United States, they are regarded as having little to no risk of default.*
>
> *The lure for investors is the interest payable on these instruments. Though interest is currently low by historical perspective, primary investors are guaranteed the return of both their interest and the principal so long as the bonds are held to their maturity.*
>
> *There are 4 types of marketable U.S. treasuries categorized primarily by their lengths of maturities:*
>
> *Treasury bills (maturing at 4, 13, 26 and 52 weeks),*
> *Treasury notes (maturing in 2, 3, 5, 7 and 10 years),*
> *Treasury bonds (which mature in 30 years), and*
> *Treasury Inflation Protected Securities (TIPS, inflation-indexed bonds offered in 5-year, 10-year and 30-year maturities).*

Marketable U.S. treasuries are issued through regularly scheduled auctions in what is called the primary market. There is also a secondary market where the already-issued securities are heavily traded by investors and primary market participants (such bonds are bought and sold through virtually any broker as well as banks and other financial institutions). This is the bond market for which we're interested for the purposes of *The 12% Solution*.

While U.S. treasuries have little to no risk of default, they do come with some risk. Treasuries are vulnerable to inflation as well as changes in interest rates. As interest rates rise, for example, primary investors who bought bonds at a lower interest rate suffer an opportunity cost. This is the cost of choosing one investment over another that would have been more profitable.

In the secondary market, these opportunity costs are factored in. Bond prices in the secondary market rise, for example, when interest rates drop and vice-versa.

What else can cause bond prices in the secondary market to rise? Fear.

Falling stock prices generally signal a loss of confidence in the economy. Whether that shaken confidence lasts a day or a week or a year, investors pulling money out of stocks will generally be seeking safer asset classes (big money abhors cash with its negligible return).

Bonds fit the bill for safety. And all that money moving out of stocks and into bonds has the effect of pushing bond prices higher. Thus, a negative correlation is born.

But higher bond prices affect the yield (interest rate return) on those bonds, driving that yield lower. As yields trend lower, bonds become less attractive from a long-term investment point of view. Thus, when stocks begin their march back up, investors are all too happy to pull out of their bonds and back into stocks – thus driving bond prices lower, yields higher, and setting bonds up to offer an attractive safe haven in the future when sentiment sours once again on stocks.

The relationship is not perfect. Any number of factors can and do drive bond prices independent of stock market sentiment. But chart the two, over the long term, and an unmistakable negative correlation – or inverse relationship -- is evident.

TLT, THE "HEDGE" TRADE

While all U.S. treasuries share that negative correlation, long-maturity bonds have price swings that most closely approximate the price swings of the overall stock market. Therefore, let's consider long bonds as the second leg of our strategy. Specifically, let's consider TLT.

Definitions:

> *__TLT__ is an ETF issued by the company iShares that tracks the Barclays U.S. 20+ Year Treasury Bond Index, a market-weighted index of bonds issued by the U.S. Treasury with remaining maturities of 20 years or more. By design, TLT is very sensitive to interest rate movements.*

Looking at the chart in Figure 1, you can see the relationship between TLT and SPY for the past 12 months. The most striking evidence of the inverse relationship can be seen in the lead-up to the June 23 U.K. referendum on whether or not Britain should withdrawal from the European Union (commonly called Brexit). See the left-hand side of the chart. The U.S. stock market, represented by SPY (in red) sold off sharply in June of 2016, while the long bonds, represented by TLT (in blue) rose sharply.

This is a good example of bonds acting as a hedge against a stock market selloff.

Notice also that as June progressed into July, investors quickly began to see the stock selloff as an overreaction and buying resumed. TLT edged downward as investors pulled money out of long-term U.S. treasuries and back into stocks.

Indeed, from a peak on July 6, 2016, TLT began a slow slide downward as worries over interest rate hikes came into play, and as stocks generally strengthened in the face of solid earnings and a U.S. political climate perceived to be positive toward business.

Figure 1

The following 2-month chart (Figure 2) shows in more detail the Brexit vote on June 23 and the immediate aftermath. You can see SPY plunging 5% that day while TLT soars by an equal amount. In the days that follow, you can see investors moving back into stocks while TLT – a bastion of the cautious - continues to post gains for a period of time.

Figure 2

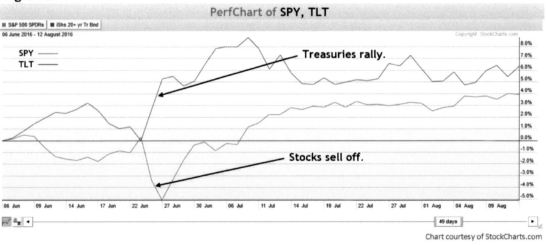

The investor who put money to work on June 6, 2016 and bought only SPY saw his account plunge by 5% just 17 days later. However, that same investor – assuming he kept himself from selling in the panic that was June 23 – managed to snag a return of

17% by year's end. The investor who bought on June 6, 2016 but split his purchase 50/50 between SPY and TLT took no hit on June 23 and was likely sipping fine wine and smoking a big cigar between bursts of braggadocio directed at his friends.

The swagger wouldn't last, however, as the hedged investor would end the year with a return of 7% (50% of SPY's gain of 17%, plus 50% of TLT's loss of 3%). Thus the cost of a hedge.

So why hedge? Why in the world would anyone go to extra lengths to make 7% on his money when a single investment in SPY generates 17%? Because the example above is just one snapshot in time. We can take snapshots all day long that show just the opposite: TLT ahead of SPY at the end of a 12-month period.

Here's a particularly good example.

Figure 3

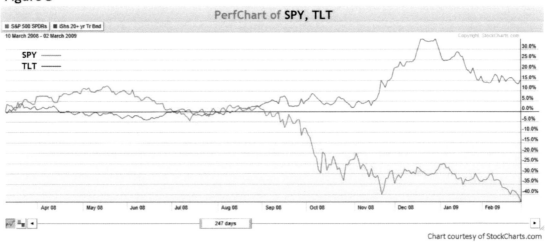

Chart courtesy of StockCharts.com

Figure 3 charts SPY and TLT for the 12 months leading up to the market bottom of The Great Recession in March of 2009. Note SPY is down 45% while TLT is up 15% for this particular 12 month period.

Taking a longer view and incorporating the 9 years to date since that market bottom in 2009, Figure 4 shows the interplay between these two ETFs during market selloffs and rallies.

Figure 4

Chart courtesy of StockCharts.com

One favorable aspect of treasuries, from a hedging point of view, is that the assets have been on a long-term uptrend. Indeed, since TLT's inception back in July 22, 2002, the ETF has generated an average annual return of 6.76%. In the past ten years, a 7.26% average annual return – actually besting the return of SPY (6.85% average annual return) during the same time frame.

Although there's usually a cost associated with the use of a hedge, not always and not for every time frame considered. In this case, a 50/50 split of SPY and TLT actually enhanced returns over a 10 year period while reducing volatility (tempering the ups and downs of the market).

Keep in mind that a long-term uptrend can always change. Past performance is no guarantee of future results.

But for now, we've made a pretty good case for using bonds as the second leg of our strategy, as the hedging component. Specifically, long-duration U.S. treasuries represented by TLT.

WHAT PERCENTAGE SPLIT?

In our recent examples, we've used a 50/50 split between SPY and TLT to provide an easy calculation. But is that the best ratio of risk asset to hedge? Turns out, it's real close. Crunching the numbers, a 60/40 mix of SPY and TLT give you a slight fractional edge over a ten-year period.

Perhaps not coincidentally, that also happens to be the ratio most cited by market analysts as the optimum mix of stocks and bonds.

Let's see what that looks like.

Figure 5 illustrates the most recent 10-year performance of a 60/40 mix of SPY and TLT. The green line marked "Backtest" is the 60/40 mix. The blue line is SPY alone functioning as a benchmark.

Figure 5 - 60/40 mix of SPY and TLT

Chart and Graphs courtesy of ETFreplay.com

Notice that the Total Return for the Backtest is slightly better than the benchmark, although this can change depending upon the particular 10-year period you are testing. Note that the Volatility is drastically reduced with the Backtest. This is due to the hedging effect of TLT and the fact that TLT frequently moves in an inverse relationship with SPY, leveling out some (but not all) of the roller coaster effect of day-to-day market moves.

So we've got the foundation laid for our strategy: a 60/40 mix of SPY and TLT. We'll be tinkering with that in the next few pages, but for now let's see how the chapter sums up.

SPY AND TLT – THE FOUNDATION
takeaways

> ➢ Collectively, the 500 stocks that make up the Standard & Poor's 500 are representative of the American stock market as a whole. Buying the ETF SPY means buying a stake in each of the 500 companies that make up the S&P 500 index.
> ➢ Buying and holding only SPY would have generated an average annual return of 7.06% over the past ten years, certainly good, but such an account would have experienced considerable volatility and a drawdown (peak-to-trough decline) of up to 45% in 2009.
> ➢ In order to hedge the risk inherent in SPY, we'll add bonds in the form of TLT, a popular ETF that tracks an index of bonds issued by the U.S. Treasury with remaining maturities of 20 years or more.
> ➢ A ratio of 60% SPY to 40% TLT is widely seen as optimal, and plays out such in backtesting.

Chapter 5 - Building on the Foundation

As we've learned, SPY is designed to track the S&P 500 stock market index. These are America's foremost large-cap stocks, and a pretty safe bet (after all, it was Warren Buffett betting on the S&P 500 in Chapter 1).

But observe the market for any length of time and you'll notice that not all U.S. stocks move up and down in unison. There are periods of time when large-cap stocks outperform small-cap stocks. Other periods when technology-heavy indexes outperform everything else (and periods when they underperform everything else). Likewise with industrial-heavy indexes.

Wouldn't it be nice if we could identify the index poised to outperform its brethren, and buy that index as the "risk-on" trade in our strategy? Then, when the outperforming index begins to lose steam and another is poised to take its place, sell the old and buy the new?

Well, that's the idea behind rotation. This is also a big hint as to where we're headed with this strategy.

Most often associated with market sectors (areas of the economy in which businesses share similar product or service, i.e. semiconductor manufacturers or consumer services companies), rotation can also be applied to broader-market indexes.

In short, the idea is that whatever sector (or index) has outperformed recently should continue to outperform for a period of time (the essence of momentum investing, confirmed by decades of data). When that time is up, another sector/index that had been out of favor will rise in the ranks to become the outperformer. The investor rotates from one to the next.

While there's certainly a case to be made for rotating in and out of sectors, we're going to stick with broader-market indices as they provide a little more stability and thus a little less volatility owing to the fact that such indices by nature are made up of more diverse businesses. Sectors, while often providing more bang for the buck, can move faster and arguably require a more hands-on trading approach than we're advocating with *The 12% Solution.*

So, which indices are we talking about? Well, the S&P 500 sets a pretty high hurdle. In order to be considered within our rotation universe, an index needs to best SPY – at least occasionally. Let's rule out world or global market indices, as well as geographic regions and national indices outside the U.S., and focus just on the U.S. market.

That still leaves quite a few, from indices based on an exchange (like NASDAQ 100 or NYSE US 100) to indices based on price-weighed or market-capitalization-weighted stocks.

With help from software provided by ETFreplay.com, I crunched out a small handful of contenders that beat SPY on occasion, and did so over the course of 10 years without negatively impacting the overall returns.

That last part is key: *without negatively impacting the overall returns.* Every index will beat the S&P 500 at one point in time or another, but keeping each of those indices in the rotation universe sometimes makes matters worse over the long term.

Why? Well, some indices are more sensitive to the kinds of economic data that renders them less predictive when compared to others. Less predictive, volatile, and fraught with reversals in short periods of time. We need indices that are relatively stable and telegraph trends in a way we can visualize and take advantage of within the parameters of *The 12% Solution.* Namely, once-a-month trading.

The following are indices that fit the bill, along with ETFs that mirror each index. Together with SPY, they will make up our rotation universe.

Definitions:

> *The NASDAQ 100 Index includes 100 of the largest domestic and international non-financial companies listed on The Nasdaq Stock Market based on market capitalization. Launched in 1985, the index reflects companies across major industry groups including computer hardware and software, telecommunications,*

retail and wholesale trade, and biotechnology. It does not contain securities of financial/investment companies. – Nasdaq.com

QQQ is a popular ETF that tracks The Nasdaq-100 Index. Managed by Invesco PowerShares.

The Russell 2000 Index is a small-cap stock market index of the bottom 2,000 stocks in the Russell 3000 Index (The Russell 3000 Index is made up of the 3,000 largest publicly held companies in America as measured by total market capitalization, and represents approximately 98% of the American public equity market). -- Wikipedia

IWM is an ETF of U.S. stocks that tracks the Russell 2000 Index. In the iShares ETF family.

The Standard & Poor's Mid-Cap 400, more commonly known as the S&P 400, is a stock market index from S&P Dow Jones Indices that include U.S. companies with a total market capitalization that ranges from $1.4 billion to $5.9 billion. The index serves as a barometer for the U.S. mid-cap equities sector, covering nearly 7 percent of the total US stock market. The index was launched on June 19, 1991. -- Wikipedia

MDY is an ETF of U.S. stocks that tracks the S&P 400 Index. In the SPDR family of funds.

Alright, so we've got our rotation candidates for the "risk-on" portion of our strategy. They are the ETFs:

- IWM
- MDY
- QQQ
- SPY

We'll be attempting to identify which one of the 4 candidates above is demonstrating the most strength relative to the others. That is, which of the 4 ETFs is outperforming. That's the one we'll buy, of course, under the assumption that outperformance begets outperformance – at least for a period of time.

WHAT PERIOD OF TIME?

And as I alluded to earlier, *The 12% Solution* involves once-a-month trading. But why not trade in and out of the contenders on the exact day in which a new leader emerges?

Markets fluctuate constantly. In trying to price thousands of assets in real time, markets (i.e., investors) succumb to all manner of trending news, crisis headlines, word-of-mouth rumors, the prognostications of analysts and talking heads, program trading and the deliberate manipulations of professional traders to manufacture market advantages.

It's largely noise and has no lasting impact on value, yet that constant noise is constantly affecting asset prices in the short run. Trying to move in and out of the contenders on the exact day in which a new leader emerges is to allow noise to control your trades. You'll end up fattening the coffers of your broker with commission fees, but not really getting ahead of the game in the end.

Putting some distance on noise -- in the form of time -- allows the truly important information to rise to the top and begin to have a more relevant impact on asset pricing. Translation: by trading once a month we filter out the noise and are better able to see the relative strength among the ETF contenders.

But why once a month? Why not once a week, or twice a month? What about quarterly or annually?

Good questions. I asked the same ones. In fact, using data partner ETFreplay.com, I crunched the charts on rotations timed bi-monthly, monthly, quarterly and annually. Turns out that monthly is the time frame that produced the highest return.

With our particular strategy, a monthly time frame filters out just enough noise-generated price swings while still capturing favorable value movements in the top-performing ETFs.

OK, we've locked in our trading schedule at once monthly. And for our particular strategy, trading on the last day of the month demonstrates a slight advantage over the first day of the month, so we'll be looking to buy the one ETF that's outperforming the others in our rotation universe on the last day of every month. But how do we determine the outperforming ETF?

Well, outperformance requires a time frame in which to judge performance. Call that the "lookback" period. If we line up a few stocks or ETFs and *look back* over a day, we can clearly see which stock or ETF outperformed its peers *for that day*. Same with a week, a month or six months – we see outperformance for that week, that month or that 6-month period.

But relative performance based on a lookback of a single day or even a week is not particularly useful to us.

With stock market assets in constant price motion, selecting a time frame in which to judge *useful* relative performance is an exercise similar to putting distance on noise. Pick too short of a time frame and noise-driven price fluctuations rule. Pick too long a time frame, and top-performing assets become less predictable for the upcoming month.

So what's the Goldilocks lookback – a time frame that's not too hot, not too cold?

Crunching the numbers with our data partner for our particular strategy, a 3-month lookback appears to be optimal. So when we are evaluating the relative performance of the ETFs in our rotation universe, we'll be using a 3-month lookback. Specifically, we'll be looking at 3-month charts.

CHARTING RELATIVE OUTPERFORMANCE

Here we come to the beauty part of the strategy: charting the relative performance of the ETFs to decide which one to invest in for the upcoming month. I say beauty part, because it's simple, it's effective, and you don't need a bunch of sophisticated software and complicated algorithms to calculate.

All you need is a stock chart that provides for simultaneously comparing multiple stocks or ETFs. And they are quite easy to find.

If you have an account with a major brokerage, you've likely got access to such charting tools. If not, they are readily available on the Web through both paid and free services. For illustration purposes, I'll be using free charts constructed from the site StockCharts.com.

Let's look at the full year 2016. For starters, Figure 6 identifies the ETF that has outperformed during a 3-month lookback period ending December 31, 2015. Remember, we buy on the last day of the month *to hold for the upcoming month*. So Figure 6 identifies the outperforming QQQ as our "risk-on" investment for January, 2016.

Figure 6 - December 31, 2015

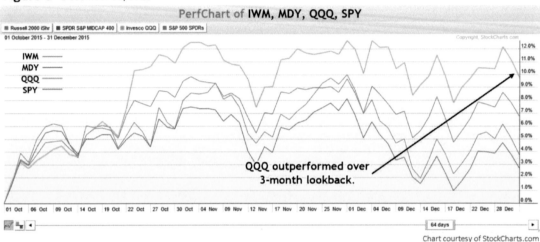

Chart courtesy of StockCharts.com

Let's move to the next month. Figure 7 identifies the ETF that has outperformed during a 3-month lookback period ending January 29, 2016. With SPY as the outperformer, that becomes our "risk-on" investment for February, 2016.

Figure 7 - January 29, 2016

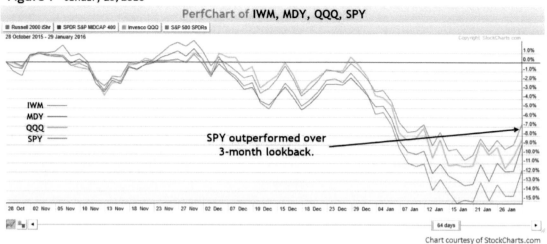

Chart courtesy of StockCharts.com

Let's move to the next month. Figure 8 identifies the ETF that has outperformed during a 3-month lookback period ending February 29, 2016. With SPY as the outperformer for the second month in a row (even though they all showed negative numbers), that remains our "risk-on" investment for March.

Figure 8 - February 29, 2016

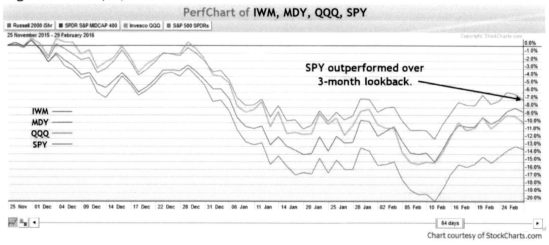

Chart courtesy of StockCharts.com

Let's do this one more time and then we'll summarize the year. Figure 9 identifies the ETF that has outperformed during a 3-month lookback period ending March 31, 2016. With MDY as the outperformer, that becomes our "risk-on" investment for April, 2016.

Figure 9 - March 31, 2016

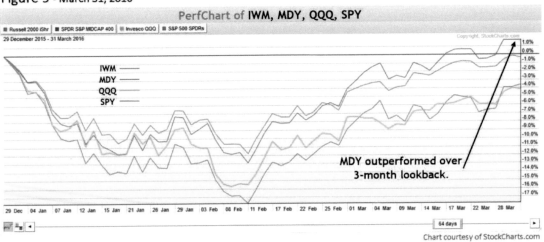

Chart courtesy of StockCharts.com

So let's see what we've got for 2016. Here's how the monthly rotation shakes out for the "risk-on" portion of our equation.

2016 "Risk-On" Rotation Table:

We buy…	For…	Which returns…	Compared to SPY…
QQQ	January	-6.91%	-4.98%
SPY	February	-0.08%	-0.08%
SPY	March	+6.72%	+6.72%
MDY	April	+1.19%	+0.39%
MDY	May	+2.25%	+1.70%
IWM	June	-0.02%	+0.35%
IWM	July	+5.87%	+3.65%
QQQ	August	+1.05%	+0.12%
IWM	September	+1.08%	+0.01%
QQQ	October	-1.46%	-1.73%
QQQ	November	+0.44%	+3.68%
IWM	December	+2.89%	+2.03%
		+13.02% Annual Return	+11.86% Annual Return

And the results of all this trading? At year's end, our strategy has returned 13.02%. Had we bought and held SPY alone, we would have seen a 11.86% return for 2016.

So for 2016, the strategy beat the benchmark – by a little. That won't happen every year. Some years it beats, some years it lags. But over time, at least over the past ten years, the strategy of buying the outperformer for the upcoming month has resulted in a significant improvement over a buy-and-hold philosophy, albeit with a slight increase in volatility and a slightly higher max drawdown.

We can see this in Figure 10. The green line, or "Backtest," is the monthly rotation of our "risk-on" ETFs played out over ten years ending in 2016. The blue line is SPY, and acts as a visual benchmark.

All told, the Backtest saw a cumulative return of 161.5% while holding SPY alone would have returned 94.3%. How does that translate into real dollars? Presuming a $10,000 initial investment, that means the Backtest would have delivered an additional $6,720 in profit over the 10 years. Were the initial investment $100,000, you'd be looking at an additional $67,200 just by applying the strategy each month for 10 years.

Note: I'm not including trading fees in this calculation, nor any tax consequences from short-term capital gains. While those variables certainly need to be taken into consideration, I think you can see that even small improvements in annual return can make a real difference in net worth over time.

Figure 10 - Monthly Rotation of "Risk-On" ETFs

Total Return (including all dividends): Dec 29, 2006 - Dec 30, 2016

Total Return %

Volatility

www.ETFreplay.com

Graphics and Stats courtesy of ETFreplay.com

Summary Statistics

	CAGR ❓	Sharpe Ratio ❓	SPY Correlation	Max Drawdn ❓
Backtest	+10.1%	0.44	+0.93	-56.3 %
SPY	+6.9%	0.32		-55.2 %

Trades ❓	115
Total Periods	120
Total Days	2518

As this is the first time we've looked at summary statistics, there are a few terms that might need explaining.

CAGR, or the Compound Annual Growth Rate, is the mean annual growth rate of an investment over a specified period of time longer than one year. *"The compound annual growth rate isn't a true return rate, but rather a representational figure. It is essentially an imaginary number that describes the rate at which an investment would have grown if it had grown at a steady rate, which virtually never happens in reality. You can think of CAGR as a way to smooth out an investment's returns so that they may be more easily understood."* -- Investopedia

The Sharpe Ratio is a formula for examining the performance of an investment or strategy by adjusting for its risk. For those into mathematics, you calculate an investment's Sharpe ratio by taking the average period return, subtracting the risk-free rate (most commonly, the 90-day Treasury bill rate), and dividing that number by the standard deviation for the period.

If all that makes your head hurt, as it does mine, here's the thing to remember: when comparing two assets or strategies against a common benchmark, the one with a higher Sharpe Ratio provides a better return for the same risk.

SPY Correlation measures the statistical relationship between an investment or strategy and the selected benchmark, in this case the S&P 500 (represented in our examples by SPY). A SPY correlation of 1.0 means that the investment or strategy in question moves in virtual lockstep with the S&P 500. A SPY correlation of 0.0 means an investment or strategy has zero relationship with the S&P 500, and price movements in one are unaffected by the other.

Max Drawdown is an indicator of downside risk over a specified time period. It measures the largest single drop from a peak to a trough in a portfolio -- before a new peak is achieved. In practical terms, it paints a worst case scenario for the investor. Maximum drawdown demonstrates how much would have been lost if an investment or strategy had been bought at its peak value, ridden all the way down, and sold at the low.

If an investment had never lost a dime, the max drawdown would be zero. If an investment lost everything, the max drawdown would be -100%.

While max drawdown is a backward-looking (historical) statistic, investors are well advised to factor it in when considering how much pain an investment has caused in the past.

BUILDING ON THE FOUNDATION
takeaways

> ➢ Not all U.S. broad market indices move in lockstep. While over time there is a tendency to converge, in shorter time frames there are outperformers and laggards. We'll take advantage of this through rotation.
> ➢ We've identified 4 indices for consideration for rotation: 1) the Russell 2000 small cap market index represented by the ETF IWM, 2) the S&P 400 mid cap market index represented by the ETF MDY, 3) the Nasdaq 100 large cap, technology-heavy index represented by the ETF QQQ, and 4) the S&P 500 large cap broad-market index represented by the ETF SPY.

> ➢ The time frame most optimal and applicable to our needs is monthly. We'll be buying on the last day of the month to hold for the upcoming month.
> ➢ The ETF candidate to buy is the one that has outperformed its peers during a "lookback" period of 3 months. With readily available charting tools, we can see which ETF has been the outperformer by charting all 4 on the same chart.
> ➢ Our backtesting confirms the advantage of index rotation over a buy-and-hold strategy.

Chapter 6 - A Cash Trigger

I'm going to do something now that – for some of you – will short circuit this book. Those 'some of you' will be tempted to read the following, nod knowingly, close the book and proceed to implement the strategy without further ado. And you'd have my blessing, because what I'm about to do will get you to *The 12% Solution*.

I'm going to show you how to implement a cash trigger.

You may have heard the expression: 'The best way to make money is to not lose it.' That's more than just a clever financial bumper sticker. It's a slogan steeped in truth. While stock market gains magnify stock market gains through the beauty of compounding returns, the reverse has a magnifying effect, too.

An example. Take a $100,000 account and lose 10%, and you're left with $90,000. Or lose 30% and you're left with $70,000. That's straightforward enough. Time to make it up through a market recovery, right? Yes, but look at the gains you'll need just to recover and get the account back up to breakeven. To go from $90,000 back to $100,000 requires an 11.1% positive return, not the 10% that caused the setback in the first place.

And to go from $70,000 back to $100,000 requires a 42.9% positive return, not the 30% that cause the setback in the first place.

In short, the greater the loss, the greater the gain has to be in order to recover the loss. And while investors are fixated with this return and that return, who's beating the S&P and which stocks are hitting all time highs, the ultimate success of any investment plan turns on one simple element: minimizing losses.

A cash trigger does this. And the implementation is quite simple. Each month, when evaluating which of the 4 "risk-on" ETFs to select for the coming period, consider exactly where that top-performer is on the graph. If it's above the "0.0%" line, that's the one you'll buy, as we've discussed. But if it is *below* the "0.0%" line, *if all the ETFs are trending below the "0.0%" line*, then you'll go to cash.

It's that simple. The zero percent line on the chart is the cash trigger.

Let's look again at Figure 7. This was the chart that dictated our "risk-on" selection for February 2016. Without the cash trigger, we would have bought SPY, as it is the out-performer of the bunch. With the cash trigger, because all ETFs – including SPY – are trending below the 0.0% line, the strategy dictates that we move to cash.

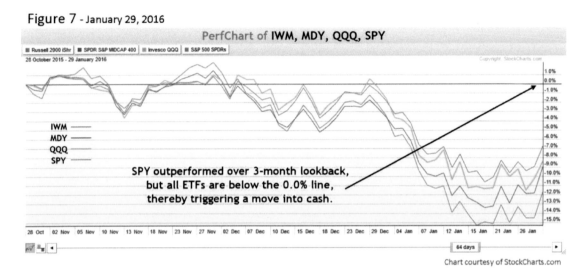

Figure 7 - January 29, 2016

Chart courtesy of StockCharts.com

How does this cash trigger impact our returns? Let's go back to 2016. Here's how the monthly rotation shakes out, both with and without the cash trigger. We buy…

Month	Without Cash Trigger	With Cash Trigger
January	QQQ	QQQ
February	SPY	SHY*
March	SPY	SHY*
April	MDY	MDY
May	MDY	MDY
June	IWM	IWM
July	IWM	IWM
August	QQQ	QQQ
September	IWM	IWM
October	QQQ	QQQ
November	QQQ	QQQ
December	IWM	IWM

* Note: Going to cash means literally "going to cash" -- selling the asset in question and simply holding cash in the account. Or, for our purposes with *The 12% Solution*, it can also mean going into SHY, the iShares 1-3 year Treasury Bond ETF which is a reasonable proxy for cash albeit with a little bit of upside potential during equity sell-offs.

Large accounts might want to consider SHY during these times, smaller accounts might not return their way out of trading fees. Investor's call.

And the results of implementing a cash trigger into our trading? At year's end (2016), our strategy with the cash trigger returned 6.3%. But wait – didn't we score a higher return without the cash trigger? Indeed, we realized a 13.02% return without the cash trigger. What in the world...?

The cash trigger failed to deliver improved results for 2016. In fact, it led to even worse results than having no such trigger, achieving exactly the opposite of what it was intended. If we go back and look at our 2016 "Risk-On" Rotation Table (p. 31), we can see the problem: going to cash (or SHY) in February and March causes us to miss out on a juicy 6.72% gain that would have been generated with SPY.

In retrospect, a study of the markets, analysts and pundits during the first few months of 2016 had all predicting an imminent market crash. To wit, this headline in Fortune Magazine: *"Analyst: Here Comes the Biggest Stock Market Crash in a Generation."* Our strategy was predicting the same, hence the move into cash. But the crash never materialized and markets rallied and it was off to the races – but without our participation for two back-to-back months. And that security blanket of cash for those two months cost us.

So the cash trigger failed us for 2016. But that was one year. And one year doesn't capture market cycles nor does it capture the entire picture of a long-term strategy. Let's backtest this and see how things would have played out over 10 years, ending in 2016.

Figure 11 gives us a chart of that time frame, incorporating the cash trigger into our monthly analysis. The green line, or "Backtest," is the monthly rotation of our "risk-on" ETFs played out over ten years ending in 2016 and includes the cash trigger. The blue line is SPY, and acts as a visual benchmark.

The arrows indicate when and where some of the more obvious cash triggers kicked in, sending us out of any "risk-on" ETF and into the loving arms of cash (or SHY, as the case may be). A month or two of an account in cash is evident by the green line going flat.

Figure 11 - Monthly Rotation of "Risk-On" ETFs with Cash Trigger

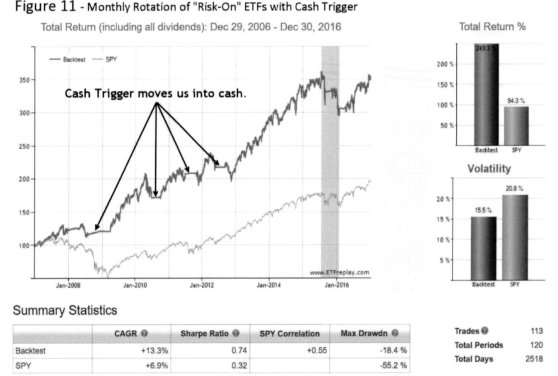

Total Return (including all dividends): Dec 29, 2006 - Dec 30, 2016

Cash Trigger moves us into cash.

www.ETFreplay.com

Total Return %

Volatility

Summary Statistics

	CAGR ❓	Sharpe Ratio ❓	SPY Correlation	Max Drawdn ❓
Backtest	+13.3%	0.74	+0.55	-18.4 %
SPY	+6.9%	0.32		-55.2 %

Trades ❓	113
Total Periods	120
Total Days	2518

Graphics and Stats courtesy of ETFreplay.com

Not only did we substantially boost the compound annual growth rate (CAGR) but we dramatically reduced both volatility and maximum drawdown by incorporating the cash trigger.

The most dramatic argument for the trigger in the above example was the year 2008. During the depth of The Great Recession while the S&P 500 crashed and burned to a negative -36.8%, our monthly ETF rotation that incorporates a simple cash trigger (first arrow, above) lost only -0.6%.

As we've seen, though, not every year is going to be a stellar year that will beat the S&P 500 benchmark. Witness 2016. But if your time horizon is 10 years plus, we've made the "risk-on" portion of our strategy a safer trade while improving overall returns. So safe, in fact, and with overall returns so improved that this will be the 'close the book' moment for some of you. And that's fine. After all, we've just generated a 13.3% CAGR on a 10-year backtest.

Stop now and be the envy of Jim Cramer. Or, keep reading and let's see what happens when we work a bond hedge into the monthly equation.

A CASH TRIGGER
takeaways

> The best way to make money is to not lose it. Or stated another way, the ultimate success of any investment plan depends on one simple element: minimizing losses. A cash trigger addresses this element.
> The zero percent line on the chart is the cash trigger. Each month, when comparing our 4 ETFs over a 3-month lookback, if all the ETFs are trending below the "0.0%" line, then the trade is to go to cash.
> While not every year sees an advantage, adding a cash trigger substantially boosts the compound annual growth rate (CAGR) over time.
> Side benefits: a cash trigger dramatically reduces both volatility and maximum drawdown.

Chapter 7 - Building on the Foundation, Part II

In Chapter 3 we laid the foundation for our strategy: a 60% to 40% mix of "risk-on" equities and bonds acting as a "hedge." We initially looked at SPY (mirroring the S&P 500 index) as our "risk-on" ETF trade and TLT (long-maturing U.S. treasuries) as our hedge.

From there, in Chapter 4, we tinkered with the "risk-on" side of the equation by moving from a buy-and-hold mindset to a monthly rotation strategy involving 4 ETFs. In Chapter 5 we added a cash trigger to the "risk-on" side of the equation in order to minimize losses during significant market downturns.

Now let's consider the "hedge" trade, the 40% of our strategy that contributes largely by reducing volatility and max drawdown of the overall investment. We had left off that discussion with TLT as our pick for a buy-and-hold hedge. Can we improve on that?

IMPROVING ON TLT

We picked TLT, the iShares ETF that tracks a market-weighted index of bonds issued by the U.S. Treasury with remaining maturities of 20 years or more, because it has a frequent negative correlation to equities (hence, the hedge), and because long-maturity treasuries have price swings that most closely approximate the price swings of the overall stock market.

But a "frequent" negative correlation doesn't mean it *always* reacts in the opposite direction of the stock market. A number of factors can and do influence U.S. Treasuries, and those influences sometimes drive the bonds in the same direction as stocks for extended periods. When this happens, treasuries lose their hedge.

And if the direction is down, losses in equities are compounded by losses in treasuries.

To try to minimize these compounded losses, we're going to approach the 40% of our strategy the same way we approached the 60% -- by considering ETF options beyond TLT, and developing a rotation schedule that switches between outperformers.

At first glance, selecting ETF alternatives beyond TLT appears daunting. One online database of ETFs (ETFDB.com) puts the number of bond ETFs at over 300 and counting. There are ETFs relating to municipal bonds, corporate bonds, emerging market bonds, government bonds (domestic and international), high-yield bonds, inflation-protected bonds, preferred stock/convertible bonds, and bonds that sample the total bond market.

But a lot of these bond ETFs duplicate one another. And most of the others are fairly easy to determine whether or not they fit our criteria: that they contribute to a rotational strategy that improves CAGR, or lowers volatility, or reduces max drawdown, or some combination of the three.

While I was hoping for a small handful of candidates from which to rotate, backtesting kept identifying a single ETF as the optimal counterweight to TLT. Consider it to be a hedge for the hedge. To the definitions.

Definitions:

> *__High-Yield Corporate Bond__ is a type of corporate bond that offers a higher rate of interest because of its higher risk of default. When companies with a greater estimated default risk issue bonds, they may be unable to obtain an investment-grade bond credit rating. As a result, they typically issue bonds with higher interest rates in order to entice investors and compensate them for this higher risk. High-yield bond issuers tend to be startup companies or capital-intensive firms with high debt ratios. -- Source: SEC*

> *JNK is an ETF that tracks the Bloomberg Barclays High Yield Very Liquid Index. In the SPDR family of funds.*

If high-yield corporate bonds have a higher risk of default, is JNK safe as an alternative to TLT? While it's true that high-yield corporate bonds (often called "junk" bonds) are riskier plays than treasuries, we have three things working in our favor.

1) JNK is an ETF, meaning that it's a basket of bonds; at last count, 959 holdings (as of 07/12/2017). As with any ETF, there's a certain safety in numbers.

2) While JNK doesn't have a 10-year track record (inception date: 11/27/2007), it does have a 9-year track record. Since that inception, the fund has averaged a 5.78% annual return vs. TLT at 6.4% for the same time frame. That's assuming a buy-and-hold, which we won't be doing. During its lifetime, it has shown a volatility number slightly lower than TLT (13.7% vs. 15.4%) and a max drawdown slightly worse (-38.5% vs. -26.6%).

3) While all junk bonds funds will react negatively to a rise in default rates, we'll be evaluating the relative strength of JNK and TLT every 30 days. That should provide us a sufficient window from which to exit if default rates begin to rise.

Alright, so we've got our rotation candidates for the "hedge" portion of our strategy. They are the ETFs:

- JNK
- TLT

As with the 60% "risk-on" portion of our strategy, we'll be attempting to identify which one of the 2 candidates above is demonstrating the most strength relative to the other. That is, which of the 2 ETFs is outperforming. That's the one we'll buy, of course, under the assumption that outperformance begets outperformance – at least for a period of time.

And as with the 60%, we'll use a month-to-month trading schedule and a lookback period of 3 months to determine relative outperformance.

CHARTING RELATIVE OUTPERFORMANCE

In keeping with our previous examples, let's look at the full year 2016. Figure 12 identifies the ETF that has outperformed during a 3-month lookback period ending December 31, 2015. Remember, we buy on the last day of the month *to hold for the upcoming month.* So Figure 12 identifies the outperforming TLT as our "hedge" investment for January, 2016.

Figure 12 - December 31, 2015

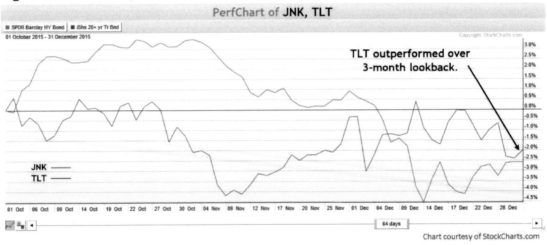

Chart courtesy of StockCharts.com

Let's move to the next month. Figure 13 identifies the ETF that has outperformed during a 3-month lookback period ending January 29, 2016. With TLT as the outperformer, that remains our "hedge" investment for February, 2016.

Figure 13 - January 29, 2016

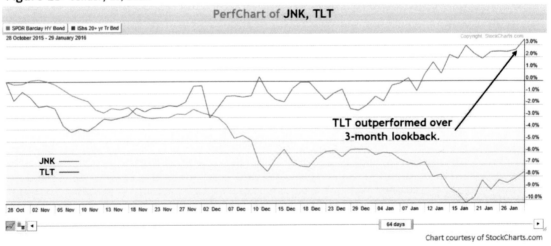

Chart courtesy of StockCharts.com

Let's move to the next month. Figure 14 identifies the ETF that has outperformed during a 3-month lookback period ending February 29, 2016. With TLT as the outperformer for the third month in a row, that remains our "hedge" investment for March, 2016.

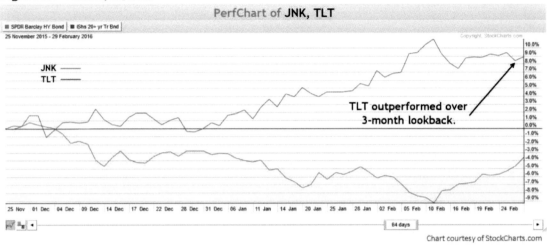

Figure 14 - February 29, 2016

Let's do this one more time and then we'll summarize the year. Figure 15 identifies the ETF that has outperformed during a 3-month lookback period ending March 31, 2016. With TLT as the outperformer, that remains our "hedge" investment for April, 2016.

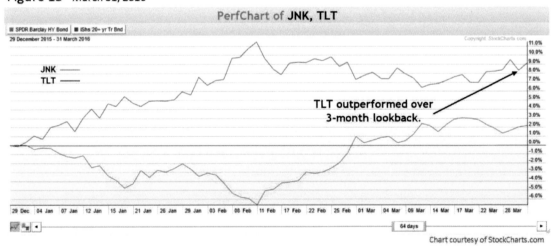

Figure 15 - March 31, 2016

So let's see what we've got for 2016. Here's how the monthly rotation shakes out for the "hedge" half of our strategy.

2016 "Hedge" Rotation Table:

We buy…	For…	Which returns…	Compared to TLT…
TLT	January	+5.57%	+5.57%
TLT	February	+3.08%	+3.08%
TLT	March	-0.09%	-0.09%
TLT	April	-0.74%	-0.74%
JNK	May	+0.32%	+0.81%
JNK	June	+1.85%	+6.93%
TLT	July	+2.10%	+2.10%
TLT	August	-1.01%	-1.01%
TLT	September	-1.51%	-1.51%
JNK	October	-0.75%	-4.38%
JNK	November	+0.13%	-8.21%
JNK	December	+1.92%	-0.46%
		+10.88% Annual Return	+2.1% Annual Return

And the result of all this trading? At year's end, the "hedge" portion of our rotational strategy has returned +10.88%. Had we bought and held TLT alone (our benchmark for the "hedge" half of the equation), we would have seen a +2.1% return for 2016. So the strategy *outperformed the TLT benchmark* for 2016.

But that was one year. And as we said before, one year doesn't capture market cycles nor does it capture the entire picture of a long-term strategy. Let's backtest this and see how things would have played out over 10 years, ending in 2016.

Figure 16 gives us a chart of that time frame. The green line, or "Backtest," is the monthly rotation of our "hedge" ETFs played out over ten years ending in 2016. The blue line is TLT, and acts as a visual benchmark.

The reason TLT is our benchmark here, and not SPY as before, is because we're currently dealing with the "hedge" portion of our strategy. TLT was our initial go-to bond fund, so if we can't beat TLT over a period of time, there's no sense in rotating among different ETFs. Thus TLT is our benchmark when it comes to the "hedge" portion of our strategy.

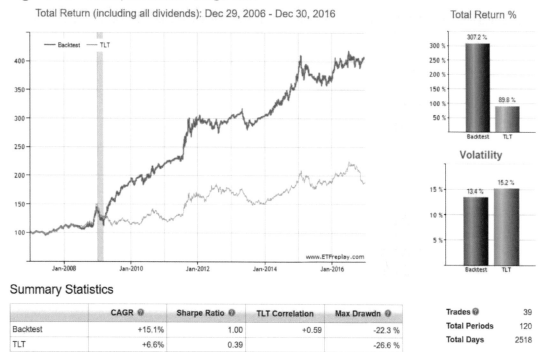

Figure 16 - Monthly Rotation of "Hedge" ETFs

Total Return (including all dividends): Dec 29, 2006 - Dec 30, 2016

Summary Statistics

	CAGR	Sharpe Ratio	TLT Correlation	Max Drawdn
Backtest	+15.1%	1.00	+0.59	-22.3 %
TLT	+6.6%	0.39		-26.6 %

Trades	39
Total Periods	120
Total Days	2518

Graphics and Stats courtesy of ETFreplay.com

Looking back over a 10-year period, not only did our rotational strategy substantially boost the compound annual growth rate (CAGR) compared to buying-and-holding TLT, but we reduced both volatility and maximum drawdown as well.

So while not every year is going to be a stellar year that will beat the TLT benchmark, if your time horizon is 10 years plus, we've made the "hedge" portion of our strategy a safer trade while improving overall returns.

BUILDING ON THE FOUNDATION, PART II
takeaways

- ➤ Given the wide diversity of bonds and the catalysts that move them, in any given time frame there are outperformers and underperformers. We'll take advantage of this through rotation.
- ➤ We've identified 2 bond types and respective ETFs for consideration: 1) the Bloomberg Barclays High Yield Very Liquid Index (corporate "junk" bonds) represented by the ETF JNK, 2) the Barclays U.S. 20+ Year Treasury Bond Index represented by the ETF TLT.
- ➤ The ETF candidate to buy is the one that has outperformed during a "look-back" period of 3 months. With readily available charting tools, we can see which ETF has been the outperformer by charting both on the same chart.
- ➤ Backtesting confirms the advantage of bond fund rotation over a buy-and-hold strategy.

Chapter 8 - The 12% Solution

From our initial nod to Warren Buffett and his simplest of plans for beating the money managers, we saw how we could improve results (or at least improve on investment risk) by swapping his Vanguard 500 Index Fund Admiral Share for a 60% to 40% mix of equities and bonds.

From there, we tinkered with multiple elements of this tried and true formula. We looked at rotating among multiple stock market indices and bond funds, and found this approach to further improve results. We identified a 3-month lookback period as the optimal history for determining which ETFs to buy, and monthly trades as most advantageous in screening out market noise.

We've seen the kind of returns generated by each segment of the equation, along with their associated volatility and max drawdown numbers. What happens when we put the pieces together into a single monthly rotational strategy?

Figure 17 shows us 10 full years of the overall strategy at work. The green line, or "Backtest," is the monthly rotation of both our "risk-on" trade and our "hedge" trade. The blue line is SPY, our benchmark.

Figure 17 - Monthly Rotation of "Risk-On" and "Hedge" ETFs (The 12% Solution)

Total Return (including all dividends): Dec 29, 2006 - Dec 30, 2016

Total Return %

Volatility

Summary Statistics

	CAGR ❓	Sharpe Ratio ❓	SPY Correlation	Max Drawdn ❓
Backtest	+14.4%	1.08	+0.36	-11.8 %
SPY	+6.9%	0.32		-55.2 %

Trades ❓	152
Total Periods	120
Total Days	2518

Graphics and Stats courtesy of ETFreplay.com

Over the most recent 10-year period, as the above Figure 17 illustrates, a monthly rotation of both our "risk-on" trade and our "hedge" trade triples our total return while cutting volatility in half and reducing our maximum drawdown by more than three fourths.

Perhaps the most compelling argument for the strategy is the year 2008. That year saw the U.S. market plummeting in the midst of The Great Recession, with the stock market finally finding a bottom in June of 2009.

Figure 18 gives the numbers: 2008 saw SPY (representative of the S&P 500) post a loss of negative -36.8%. Conversely, our strategy returned a positive +10.9% that same year.

Figure 18 - Annual Performance of The 12% Solution for 10 years

Year	Total Return	SPY Total Return	+ / -	Max Draw Down	SPY Max Draw Dn
2007	+17.5%	+5.1%	+12.4%	-6.0%	-9.9%
2008	+10.9%	-36.8%	+47.7%	-11.4%	-47.6%
2009	+43.4%	+26.4%	+17.0%	-8.9%	-27.1%
2010	+12.1%	+15.1%	-3.0%	-11.8%	-15.7%
2011	+15.9%	+1.9%	+14.0%	-6.0%	-18.6%
2012	+3.5%	+16.0%	-12.5%	-11.7%	-9.7%
2013	+21.6%	+32.3%	-10.7%	-6.7%	-5.6%
2014	+17.6%	+13.5%	+4.1%	-3.5%	-7.3%
2015	-1.5%	+1.3%	-2.8%	-8.4%	-11.9%
2016	+8.5%	+12.0%	-3.5%	-6.2%	-10.3%

Annual Performance courtesy of ETFreplay.com

At the same time, you can see that the strategy doesn't beat the overall market every year, something I've tried to stress throughout this book. Some years it outperforms, other years it lags. But overall, taken with a longer term outlook, the strategy beats the market and does so with less risk and less of a roller coaster ride.

Let's pull it all together and summarize the mechanics of our strategy that generates average annual returns of 12%. Actually, we generated 14.4% annually as per Figure 17, but I like 12% because it's conservative. I'd rather under promise and over deliver than the other way around.

So, here's how it works…

THE "RISK-ON" TRADE

Once a month, on the last day of the month, we will chart the relative performance of 4 index ETFs to decide which one to invest in for the upcoming month. The ETFs for our "risk-on" trade are as follows: IWM, MDY, QQQ, SPY.

We chart their relative performance by using an online stock chart that provides for simultaneously comparing multiple stocks or ETFs – either the stock chart that is incorporated on the Web pages of your brokerage account, or one that is readily available through both paid and free Web services. For illustration purposes throughout this book, I've used free charts constructed from the site StockCharts.com (specifically, their "Perf Charts").

Once the ticker symbols of the 4 ETFs are entered into the chart, and a 3-month time frame selected, the outperforming ETF will become evident: it's the one whose graph line is uppermost on the chart as of today's date. That's the ETF we will buy to hold for the following month until the process repeats on the last day of the following month.

As this represents our "risk-on" trade, it commands 60% of the account (or 60% of the amount you allocate for the strategy). So, we'll allocate 60% to this fund.

IMPORTANT REMINDER: Should none of the graph lines make it above the 0.0% line, this portion of our account (or strategy allocation) goes to cash. This is called our cash trigger, and helps to prevent large losses in the "risk-on" trade. So before selecting the outperformer of the bunch, make sure it is above the 0.0% line. Otherwise, hold cash in 60% of your account.

THE "HEDGE" TRADE

Once we've finished with our "risk-on" trade, we'll turn our attention to the "hedge" portion of our strategy. Using the same comparative chart, we'll remove the equity ETF ticker symbols and replace them with the ticker symbols for our 2 bond funds, namely JNK and TLT.

We'll repeat the same process, and select the outperforming bond ETF for the 3-month lookback period. That's the ETF we'll buy to hold for the coming month until the process repeats.

As this represents our "hedge" trade, we'll allocate 40% to this fund.

NOTE: No need for a cash trigger here, as backtesting has shown no advantage. Which makes sense, as the very definition of a hedge is an investment that reduces the risk of adverse price movements in an asset.

In the event relative performance testing determines that we keep the same ETF(s) as the previous month, then the only trade necessary is that which rebalances to maintain a 60/40 mix of "risk-on" and "hedge" investments. And if the imbalance is slight? Forget rebalancing, save the trading commissions, and just let the ETFs ride.

AND THEN?

Once the trades are executed, step away from the computer and try not to let the daily market noise lure you into further trading. Approach it once a month, make the trades dictated by the strategy, then let the strategy do the heavy lifting. The results we've shown through backtesting are predicated on once-monthly trading. To trade more frequently or less frequently is to strip the strategy of its value.

Trade once a month, then go live your life.

Chapter 9 - OK, But Does an Extra 5% Really Matter?

This book lays out a plan for achieving a 12% annual return – on average – in the stock market. The skeptic might say that one can already achieve 7% with no effort whatsoever (or more precisely, 7.1% as per Warren Buffett's mutual fund choice in Chapter 3). And by 'no effort whatsoever,' the skeptic means buy-and-hold. Buy one mutual fund, hold it, boom: 7.1% average annual return over ten years.

So why, asks the skeptic, should we give up that bird in the hand in return for a lousy 5% extra per year? Especially when that extra 5% requires us to pull ourselves away from the television for 20 minutes per month to execute big league trades on the frightening web pages of a discount stock broker?

Indeed. What difference does 5% make in the grand scheme of things? And is it worth the trouble? Well, let's load the following table with some data.

	Warren Buffett's Mutual Fund Choice	The 12% Solution
Starting Balance	$5,000	$5,000
Annual Contributions	$1,200	$1,200
Years Contributed	40	40
Annual Return	7.1%	12.0%

Let's assume we're starting with an investment of $5,000. To that initial investment, we're adding $100 per month, or $1,200 per year. Let's also assume we're young and hip and happening, and we've got 40 years to play around with this. Yes, 40 years is a long time. But if you're 25 years old now, 40 years puts you at age 65. Consider this a retirement plan. The annual returns we've plugged in are backtested returns for the previous 10 years.

As we've learned, past performance is no guarantee of future results, but we've got to go with something.

We're comparing Warren Buffett's choice of mutual funds (buying and holding the Vanguard 500 Index Fund Admiral Share,) with *The 12% Solution*. The difference in annual return is almost 5% (technically, 4.9%). So how does that 4.9% difference stack up over the years?

Year	Warren Buffett's Mutual Fund Choice	The 12% Solution
2017	$5,000.00	$5,000.00
2022 (plus 5 years)	$13,962.26	$16,435.13
2027 (plus 10 years)	$26,586.32	$36,587.72
2032 (plus 15 years)	$44,377.94	$72,103.49
2037 (plus 20 years)	$69,448.42	$134,694.40
2042 (plus 25 years)	$104,775.68	$245,000.97
2047 (plus 30 years)	$154,555.97	$439,398.83
2052 (plus 35 years)	$224,702.26	$781,994.29
2057 (plus 40 years)	$323,546.66	$1,385,764.56

At the end of 40 years, following *The 12% Solution* and the assumptions we made earlier delivers an additional $1,062,217.90 to your account. That 4.9% annual difference means you're a millionaire at the end of the exercise. Without the 4.9%? Not so much.

Note that we're not accounting for trading fees and commission, nor any additional tax bite for claiming short-term vs. long-term capital gains (for those trading in a traditional, taxable brokerage account). These certainly need to be taken into consideration. But I think you'll agree we're still talking about a significant difference in the payday at the end of 40 years.

Let's look at it another way. Take that additional $1,062,217.90 generated by the strategy and divide that by 40 (as in years) and you get $26,555.44. That's the income you'll be receiving for each of the 40 years that you work the strategy. Having put up $5,000 *just once*, and then adding $100 per month to your account, the strategy returns over $26,000 a year.

That's like having a second job that requires 20 minutes of work per month and pays $26,000 a year. Of course there's one condition: you've got to wait 40 years for the payday.

So what difference does 5% make in the grand scheme of things? And is it worth the trouble? Each prospective investor will have to decide that for themselves.

To those who see the difference, decide it's worth the trouble, *and have patience*, I wish you wealth.

///

Note from the Author:

I am offering a monthly service that does the chart work for *The 12% Solution*, and provides readers with the resulting buy/sell signals via email. It's a free service to purchasers of this book.

Also included with signup, a link to strategy updates and FAQs that have accumulated since the date of publication.

Signup at the following location:

https://www.DavidAlanCarter.com/12signup

Use Password: 12key

Chapter 10 - Caveats and Q&A

From the beginning, I wanted to create a trading system that could hold its own against the benchmark S&P 500 Index, while offering reduced risk in the form of volatility and drawdowns. I wanted a model that was not only transparent (I wanted to see the mechanisms at work), but one that made a certain intuitive, logical sense. And finally, I wanted something that was easy to implement; something that would reduce to a minimum the difficult decision making that is inherent with investing.

I sleep better at night with this strategy at work in my portfolio. I hope you will, too.

That said, no mechanical trading system is perfect, and certainly not this one. There will be years that it beats the benchmark, and years that it will underperform. The composite results we achieved are due in no small part by the extended time frame over which we conducted the backtests.

That time frame, 10 years, included a major market crash and bear market, and a number of smaller crises and selloffs, allowing the built-in cash trigger to kick in and protect profits even as the strategy gave up some of those profits in bullish years.

Which leads to the first caveat...

CAVEAT #1 – THE MODEL MAY NOT WORK AS A SHORT-TERM STRATEGY. Not every year sees a significant correction, but practically every year delivers multiple threats of such a correction – head fakes and false signals, times when the market appears to be moving in one direction only to end up reversing course and moving in the other.

The model was designed with an ever-present bond allocation to help smooth out volatility, and with a cash trigger to further protect during corrections. But in order for that cash trigger to do its job, it must necessarily kick into gear during any number of *threats* of corrections. That means sometimes sitting out markets that end up moving higher.

In that respect, one or two or three years of underperformance should not be used as an indictment against the strategy. Protection is at the strategy's core.

CAVEAT #2 – NOT EVERY MARKET MOVE DOWNWARD WILL HAVE PROTECTION. The strategy will not protect during flash crashes or steep losses that play out over a period of several days.

Why? In large part because the strategy only rebalances once a month. The strategy ignores interim gyrations of the market. A mid-month event like a sudden plunge in stocks that individual investors might act on out of emotion (for better or worse) would find cold reception in the strategy.

These are not itchy fingers on a sell button. The decision to sell (or buy) is calculated only once a month. So to be honest, a market crash that begins on the second day of the month can take a portfolio down any number of percentage points before the strategy decides to "go to cash" on the last trading day of that month. That action might protect going forward, if the move that month was a precursor to a more serious downturn (and not a head fake). But damage to one's portfolio could still be significant.

That's the max drawdown we keep talking about. Historically (for the past 10 years), it's been as great as -11.8%. But there's no guarantee it can't go higher in the future. So, just a heads up.

Questions & Answers

///

Q 3 Calendar Months, Or Trading Days Only? The lookback period is 3 months. Is that literally 3 calendar months, or trading days only?

A The strategy uses trading days. The NYSE and NASDAQ average about 252 trading days a year. Therefore, 3 months is 252/4 = 63 trading days.

Most charts with a "3 Month" button will calculate that time frame according to the above mathematics. If you're using a charting service that requires you to plug in the actual number of days, use 64. That will give you the 63-day *return* we need for the lookback.

///

Q Trade At Open, Close, Or Sometime In Between? On the last trading day of the month, are we placing trades at the open, the close, or somewhere in between?

A The strategy executes trades at the close of the last trading day of the month. It's those closing prices it uses in its profit/loss calculations. So, technically, the strategy is looking back 3 months (63 trading days) from the market close of the last trading day of the month.

That may seem difficult to emulate. Here's what I do. I either place my trades an hour or two prior to close on that last trading day, or I wait until the next day – the first trading day of the next month. Usually the latter.

There's wiggle room in the strategy. Executing trades within a day or two of the strategy's timing will result in a fractional difference in your average annual returns vs. the strategy's. But that might be to the slight upside or the slight downside.

///

Q Cash Trigger On The Hedge Side? I'm concerned about the performance of bond funds in a rising interest rate environment. What if TLT and JNK stop providing a hedge? Wouldn't a cash trigger add an element of safety?

A A cash trigger on the hedge side *should* add an extra element of safety. That seems logical. The problem is, that element of safety didn't exactly play out in backtesting. When I ran that scenario over 10 years, it actually reduced returns (a little bit) with no significant benefit to max drawdown or volatility.

But that's looking backward (the only direction the strategy can look). Going forward, as you suggest, we might find ourselves in a rising inflation environment which will test bonds ability to provide a hedge. Might a cash trigger be justified in the future? Rather than wait for backtesting to answer that question, concerned investors could consider adding such a trigger on the hedge side. Just understand that the [backtested] data doesn't support a benefit.

///

Q   Two Books, Two Strategies. Is this the same cash trigger that you discuss in your other book, **Stock Market Cash Trigger**?

A   It is not. They are two different methodologies. Why? *The 12% Solution* is a tightly-focused model with minimal moving parts and an ever-present bond component.

What worked for *The 12% Solution* wasn't necessarily optimal for trying to protect risk assets outside of that model, from the vast array of ETFs to individual stocks. Adjustments were necessary. Hence, the **Stock Market Cash Trigger**.

///

Q   Capital Gains Taxes. Because we're potentially trading monthly, do you have any advice for managing capital gains taxes?

A   Each investor's situation will be different, so I can't presume to offer blanket advice except to say that tax implications should always be a consideration with any system that trades more frequently than annually. That said, two things:

If you limit trades to a tax-deferred or tax-free retirement account, you won't be taxed for capital gains along the way (taxes are due on withdrawals with the former, and avoided altogether with the latter).

If you must trade in a traditional (taxable) brokerage account, you'll need to determine whether a potential 5% annual improvement in your portfolio justifies the increased burden of paying short-term capital gains taxes on those returns. In other words, whether the benefits of *The 12% Solution* are outpacing the tax man.

///

More Questions? See FAQs that have accumulated since the date of publication by signing up for the free monthly alerts. See "**A Note To The Reader**" for information.

A Note To The Reader

Thank You

Thank you for reading *The 12% Solution*. I sincerely hope you found it a contribution to your investment goals.

Gaining exposure as an independent author relies mostly on word-of-mouth, so if you have the time and inclination, please consider leaving a short review on Amazon or Goodreads. Your thoughts are important and I would be honored to have you share them.

-- David Alan Carter

Sign Up for Monthly Trade Alerts

As previously mentioned, I'm offering a monthly service that does the chart work for *The 12% Solution*, and provides readers with the resulting buy/sell signals via an email newsletter. It's free to purchasers of this book.

Also included with signup, a link to strategy updates and FAQs that have accumulated since the date of publication.

Signup at the following location:

https://www.DavidAlanCarter.com/12signup

Use Password: 12key

About The Author

Growing up in the Southern Great Plains region, author David Alan Carter was taught from an early age to work hard and protect what you've got. The former came naturally. The latter, protecting what you've got (i.e. money), took some twists and turns throughout the years before he finally got the hang of it.

One particularly gut-wrenching turn: The Great Recession, when his stock portfolio plunged along with the hopes and dreams of millions of American families.

"That was a watershed moment," Carter recalls. "Like so many others impacted, my attitude toward investing would be forever changed."

Cut to present day 2017. With almost 20 years of investing experience ranging from buy-and-hold to swing trading to high-frequency day trading, Carter has distilled those lessons learned into simple, testable and repeatable trading strategies that can benefit anyone interested in making money – and keeping money – in the stock market.

The 12% Solution is the first in a coming series on investing and personal finance.

_____

Trader
Author, Publisher, former Newspaper Columnist
Bachelors in Business Management, Oklahoma State University

Also by the author...
Stock Market Cash Trigger

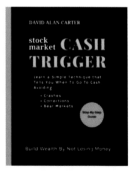

Also By David Alan Carter

STOCK MARKET CASH TRIGGER

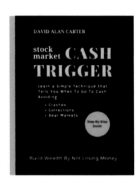

If you're holding individual stocks or ETFs, are you prepared for the next 2008?

STOCK MARKET CASH TRIGGER presents an easy, do-it-yourself technique that tests once a month to see if your individual stocks or funds are in jeopardy of a broader market selloff. If so, it provides actionable trade recommendations that have delivered a 17-year history of beating a buy-and-hold model.

Yes, there is a "cash trigger" embedded within the confines of *The 12% Solution*. And that works quite well for protecting the small universe of 4 risk assets in that strategy. But the author was searching for a mechanism better suited for protecting a broad diversity of *individual* stocks and ETFs from the ravages of market bears and bursting bubbles. And he found it. Find it for yourself.

Check It Out On Amazon.

Appendix A: Brokers and Commissions

If you're new to stock market investing, you'll need to set up and fund an account with a stock broker in order to buy and sell ETFs. While the mechanics of that is beyond the scope of this book, I wanted to take a moment to address brokers in general and their trading commissions relating to ETFs.

Brokers can be broadly categorized into Full Service and Discount/Online. Because you'll be identifying the ETFs you wish to buy and sell each month, there is little need for a Full Service Broker. These companies specialize in providing personalized service and investment recommendations for their clients – and they charge accordingly.

Save yourself the big bucks and learn how to execute buy and sell orders. That way you can take advantage of Discount/Online Brokers. The learning process is straightforward, and every Discount/Online Broker has online tools to educate you and guide you through the process.

Know that competition is fierce among the online brokers. Trading commissions have dropped into the $4.95 to $6.95 range with a number of the major online brokers. Even better, there is a trend to offer commission free trades on select ETFs. This is certainly worthwhile to investigate, since commissions and fees can erode investable funds and returns.

But be careful: not all online brokers that offer commission-free ETF trades have terms suitable to our needs. For example, many such trades are commission free only if you hold the ETF for an extended period. To sell before that date is to incur *magnified* commissions, sometimes $20 or more.

This is called an early-redemption fee, and in smaller accounts they can suck the life out of returns pretty quickly.

Here's a quick overview of some of the leading discount/online brokerage firms and their policies regarding commission-free ETF trades. Terms can and do change, so check the current status with any prospective broker before signing up.

Remember, all brokers will let you trade ETFs for a commission. The following is information regarding *commission-free trades* on select ETF.

Charles Schwab

- <u>Offers</u>: Over 200 ETFs with zero trading commissions.
- <u>Early Redemption Fee</u>: None.
- <u>Enrollment</u>: None.
- <u>Summary</u>: Schwab ETF OneSource offers over 200 ETFs with no trading commissions and no early redemption fees. That's the good news. The bad news? Those 200+ ETFs include none of the ETFs on our monthly rotation list. Yes, there are available ETFs that are vaguely similar in makeup to most on our list, both proprietary to Schwab and from 3rd party providers. But in keeping with the axiom "there is no free lunch," don't be surprised to find higher net expense ratios associated with "OneSource" ETFs, as well as thinner trading volumes that can sometimes lead to investors paying fractionally higher prices than they otherwise might in comparable ETFs with higher trading volumes. You'll need to weigh the pros and cons of "commission-free" trades with Schwab's ETF OneSource.

E*Trade

- <u>Offers</u>: Over 100 ETFs with zero trading commissions.
- <u>Early Redemption Fee</u>: Yes, up to $19.99.
- <u>Enrollment</u>: None.
- <u>Summary</u>: No trading commissions on 100+ ETFs. That's the good news. The bad news? Sell one of those ETFs in less than 30 days and you'll incur a "short-term trading fee" of $19.99. Note: None of E*Trade's commission-free ETFs match the ones on our monthly rotation list. Yes, there are available ETFs that are vaguely similar in makeup to most on our list. But as per Schwab, don't be surprised to find higher net expense ratios as well as thinner trading volumes on some of these alternatives. You'll need to weigh the pros and cons of "commission-free" trades with E*Trade.

TD Ameritrade

- <u>Offers</u>: Over 100 ETFs with zero trading commissions.
- <u>Early Redemption Fee</u>: Yes, $19.99.
- <u>Enrollment</u>: Required.
- <u>Summary</u>: No trading commissions on 100+ ETFs, two of which match the ones on our monthly rotation list (the bond funds JNK and TLT). That's the good news. The bad news? Sell one of those ETFs in less than 30 days and you'll incur a "short-term trading fee" of $19.99. Note: The remaining ETFs on our monthly rotation list are not included among TD Ameritrade's commission-free ETFs. Yes, there are available ETFs that are vaguely similar in makeup to most on our list. But don't be surprised to find higher net expense ratios as well as thinner trading volumes on any alternative. You'll need to weigh the pros and cons of "commission-free" trades with TD Ameritrade.

Fidelity

- <u>Offers</u>: Over 90 ETFs with zero trading commissions.
- <u>Early Redemption Fee</u>: Yes, up to $12.95.
- <u>Enrollment</u>: None.
- <u>Summary</u>: No trading commissions on 90+ ETFs, including 70 funds from the world's leading ETF provider, iShares. One of these funds matches the ones on our monthly rotation list (the bond funds TLT). That's the good news. The bad news? Sell TLT in less than 30 days and you'll incur a "short-term trading fee" of up to $12.95. Note: The remaining ETFs on our monthly rotation list are not included among Fidelity's commission-free ETFs. Yes, there are available ETFs that are vaguely similar in makeup to most on our list. But don't be surprised to find higher net expense ratios as well as thinner trading volumes on any alternative. You'll need to weigh the pros and cons of "commission-free" trades with Fidelity.

I've only included 4 of the leading brokerage firms offering commission-free ETF trades. There are others you can explore.

Remember, even though a brokerage firm doesn't have the ETF you want on their commission-free list, you can still buy and sell the fund (albeit for a commission).

You'll have to decide whether it's worth trading alternatives to the ETFs we selected for our monthly rotation in order to snag free commissions.

If you're tempted, start by comparing 1, 3 and 5-year returns for both your target ETF and the commission-free alternative. Your broker should have such information on their research pages. If not, such information is accessible on multiple free sites such as Yahoo Finance (https://finance.yahoo.com).

And while commission-free trades are certainly nice, watch out for those early-redemption fees.

Appendix B: Disclaimer

No Financial Advice

The entire contents of this book and any associated media (website, newsletter, email alert service, etc.), are provided for educational, informational, and entertainment purposes only. We (the author, editors and publishers) are not securities brokers or dealers and we are not financial advisers, analysts or planners. We are neither licensed nor qualified to provide investment advice. The information contained within this book is not an offer to buy or sell securities. Nothing within these pages or on associated media takes into account the particular investment objectives, financial situations, or needs of individuals, therefore should not be construed as a personal recommendation. WE ARE NOT SOLICITING ANY ACTION.

Do Your Own Due Diligence

The information provided is not intended as a complete source of information on any particular company, investment, asset or market. An individual should never make investment decisions based solely on information contained within our book or any associated media (or any book or website, for that matter). Readers should assume that all information regarding companies, investments, assets or markets is not trustworthy unless verified by their own independent research.

Investing In Securities Is High Risk

Any individual who chooses to invest in any securities should do so with caution. Investing in securities is inherently speculative and carries a high degree of risk; you may lose some or all of the money that is invested, and if you engage in margin transactions your loss may exceed the amount invested. Before acting on any analysis, advice, trade triggers or recommendations, investors should consider whether the security or strategy in question is suitable for their particular circumstances and, if necessary, seek professional advice. You must decide your own suitability to trade. YOU ASSUME ALL RISKS AND COSTS ASSOCIATED WITH ANY TRADING YOU CHOOSE TO TAKE.

Past Performance No Guarantee

Trading results can never be guaranteed. The information provided in this book and associated media regarding the past performance of any security or strategy is only representative of historical conditions in the marketplace, and is not to be construed as a guarantee that such conditions will exist in the future or that such performance will be achieved in the future. The price and value of investments referred to in this book and any associated media, and the income from them may go down as well as up, and investors may realize losses on any investments. Past performance is no guarantee of future results. Future returns are not guaranteed, and a loss of original capital may occur. ONLY INVEST WITH MONEY THAT YOU CAN AFFORD TO LOSE.

Differences in Portfolio Performance

Readers should be aware that numerous variables including timing of trade, trading commission, slippage and execution issues, may result in actual portfolio performance to differ measurably from modeled and backtested strategy performance.

Reliability Of Data

The contents of this book and any associated media -- text, graphics, links and other materials -- are based on public information that we consider reliable, but we do not represent that it is accurate or complete, and it should not be relied on as such. This book and associated media may contain inaccuracies, typographical errors and other errors. All information and materials are provided on an "as is" and "as available" basis, without warranty or condition of any kind either expressed or implied. The author does not warrant the quality, accuracy, reliability, adequacy or completeness of any of such information and material, and expressly disclaims any liability for errors or omissions in such information and material. Opinions expressed herein are the author's opinions as of the date of publication of those opinions, and may or may not be updated.

No Warranties

The 12% Solution does not guarantee or warrant the quality, accuracy, completeness, timeliness, appropriateness or suitability of the information or of any product or services referenced. The author assumes no obligation to update the information or advise on further developments concerning topics mentioned. This book may contain links to Internet sites. Such links are provided for reference only and were independently developed by parties other than the author. We are not responsible for the contents of any such linked sites and do not assume any responsibility for the accuracy or appropriateness of the information contained at such sites. The inclusion of any link does not imply endorsement by the author of the site. Use of any such linked site is at the user's own risk.

Additional Risk Disclosure Statement for System Trading

The 12% Solution develops a rules-based portfolio investment strategy that makes extensive use of hypothetical or simulated performance results. Pursuant to the Commodity Futures Trading Commission (CFTC) Rule 4.41(b): Hypothetical or simulated performance results have certain inherent limitations. Unlike an actual performance record, simulated results do not represent actual trading. Also, since the trades have not actually been executed, the results may have under- or over-compensated for the impact, if any, of certain market factors, such as lack of liquidity.

One of the limitations of hypothetical performance results is that they are generally prepared with the benefit of hindsight. In addition, hypothetical trading does not involve financial risk, and no hypothetical trading record can completely account for the impact of financial risk in actual trading. For example, the ability to withstand losses or adhere to a particular trading program in spite of trading losses are material points which can also adversely affect actual trading results.

There are numerous other factors related to the markets in general or to the implementation of any specific trading program which cannot be fully accounted for in the preparation of hypothetical performance results and all of which can adversely affect actual trading results. NO REPRESENTATION IS BEING MADE THAT ANY ACCOUNT WILL OR IS LIKELY TO ACHIEVE PROFIT OR LOSSES SIMILAR TO THOSE SHOWN.

We Will Not Be Liable

To the fullest extent of the law, we (the author, editors and publishers) will not be liable to any person or entity for the quality, accuracy, completeness, reliability, or timeliness of the information provided within this book and associated media, or for any direct, indirect, consequential, incidental, special or punitive damages whatsoever and howsoever caused, that may arise out of or in connection with the use or misuse of the information we provide. Such referenced "damages" may include, but not be limited to, lost profits, loss of opportunities, trading losses, or damages that may result from any inaccuracy or incompleteness of this information, whether such damages arise in contract, tort, strict liability, negligence, equity or statute law or by way of any other legal theory. We disclaim any liability for unauthorized use or reproduction of any portion of the information from this book or associated media.

Consent and Agreement

Please be advised that your continued use of this book or the information provided herein or with any associated media shall indicate your consent and agreement to these terms.